IIO632468

TAKE AND EAT

Bible Stories for Kids about the Eucharist

JARED DEES

Scripture texts in this work are based on the New Revised Standard Version Bible, copyright © 1989 the Division of Christian Education of the National Council of the Churches of Christ in the United States of America. Used by permission. All rights reserved.

———————————————————

© 2020 Jared Dees

All rights reserved.
No part of this book may be reproduced or used in any manner without written permission of the copyright owner except for the use of quotations in a book review.

For more information visit jareddees.com.

Paperback: ISBN 978-1-7332048-6-6
eBook: ISBN 978-1-7332048-7-3

First Edition

CONTENTS

AN INTRODUCTION FOR PARENTS

I invite you to take a journey with young people through this series of stories from the Old and New Testament about the Eucharist. *Eucharist* is a word that means "thanksgiving" in Greek. We give thanks when we celebrate the Eucharist. The stories you will read in this book will also fill children with a sense of thanksgiving for the sacrificial death and resurrection of God's only Son, Jesus Christ.

The Old Testament stories in this collection, beginning with the Original Sin in Genesis and continuing with the stories of Moses and the Israelites, prefigure the Eucharist. They find fulfillment in the Last Supper and Jesus's death and resurrection that we celebrate on Sundays.

The New Testament stories you will find here give context to the unity we experience when we eat the Body and Blood of Christ. You will read stories about what Jesus said and did during his ministry. You will find stories about how the early Church understood the "breaking of the bread" in the Acts of the Apostles, Saint Paul's writings, and the book of Revelation.

It is my goal that by reading these stories, young people will gain a greater appreciation for Christ's presence in the Eucharist today. I hope that they think of these stories as they listen to the prayers at Mass. I pray that experiencing these stories will allow them to experience a true encounter with the living God in the Eucharist.

AN INTRODUCTION FOR CHILDREN

A miracle happens every time we go to Mass. You may not notice it. You may not see anything change up on the altar as the priest raises the bread and wine toward heaven, but I assure you that it is a miracle. The Bible stories in this book will help you understand the meaning of this miracle.

The Old Testament tells the story of God's people from the beginning of time up to the time of Jesus. There are many stories in the Old Testament about bread and sacrificial food. Reading these stories will help you understand why Jesus instituted the Eucharist during the Last Supper.

The New Testament includes stories about Jesus and the first Christians. After Jesus died, rose, and ascended into heaven, Christians gathered together for the "breaking of the bread." They celebrated a feast of bread and wine, just as Jesus instructed them to do during the Last Supper. It is this very same feast that we celebrate today during Mass.

The stories in this book will help you understand the meaning and significance of the celebration of communion. Whether you are preparing for your first communion or already able to receive the Eucharist, I pray that the Lord will open your heart as you read so that you can experience his love in new ways through the sacred celebration of his Blessed Sacrament.

THE FOOD OF THE FIRST SIN

Genesis 3

The first sin in the Bible has to do with eating. Jesus gave Adam and Eve one rule, and they broke it.

As you read this story, pay attention to the punishment Adam and Eve must suffer as a result of their sin.

God created Adam and Eve and placed them in the beautiful Garden of Eden. In that garden, there were many trees. One of these trees was the Tree of Life. As long as they ate from this tree, they would never die.

There was another tree in the middle of the garden that God commanded Adam not to eat. It was called the Tree of Knowledge of Good and Evil.

"You may eat of every tree in the garden, but you shall not eat of the Tree of Knowledge of Good and Evil, or you will die," God commanded them.

But the serpent, who was Satan, approached Eve as she stood near the Tree of Knowledge. "Did God really say not to eat from any tree in the garden?" he asked her.

"We may eat the fruit of the trees in the garden, but God told us not to eat of this tree, or we will die," she told the serpent.

"You will not die!" said the serpent. "God knows that when you eat it, your eyes will be opened and you will be like gods, knowing good and evil."

Eve looked at the fruit of the tree. It looked very tasty. She plucked a fruit and ate it. Then she gave some to her husband, Adam, who was with her. He ate the fruit, too.

They tried to hide from God, but he came and found them. "Where are you?" God asked. "Have you eaten from the tree which I commanded you not to eat?"

They were ashamed.

"Because you have done this, you shall work hard to produce food all the days of your life. By the sweat on your forehead, you shall make bread to eat until you return to the ground and are buried after your death."

REFLECTION QUESTIONS

What punishments did Adam and Eve have to suffer for eating of the Tree of Knowledge?

What would humans eat after this sin?

How does it feel when you disobey parents or teachers?

THE BLESSING OF MELCHIZEDEK

Genesis 14:17–20

In the New Testament book of Hebrews, Jesus is described as a "priest forever according to the order of Melchizedek" (Hebrews 7:17, quoting Psalm 110:4). Melchizedek appears only briefly in the book of Genesis, but he was looked upon by Jews and Christians for centuries with great honor.

As you read this story, pay attention to what Melchizedek brings with him to bless Abraham.

Abram, whom God later renamed Abraham, went into battle to rescue his nephew Lot. He won the battle, saved his nephew, and then returned home.

Melchizedek was the king and high priest of Salem, which is now the city of Jerusalem. He came to bless Abram after the battle. He brought with him bread and wine. He blessed Abram with these words:

"Blessed be Abram by God Most High, maker of heaven and earth; and blessed be God Most High, who has delivered your enemies into your hand."

After the blessing, Abram gave the high priest one tenth of all the riches he had won during the battle.

REFLECTION QUESTIONS

How are Melchizedek's offering and Jesus Christ's offering similar?

What are some of the things you can ask God to bless today?

Abram gave the high priest 10 percent of everything he won in the battle. How can you donate some of your money or time to the Church?

THE SACRIFICE OF ISAAC

Genesis 22:1–19

One of the most famous Bible verses in the New Testament is John 3:16, which says, "For God so loved the world that he gave his only Son, so that everyone who believes in him may not perish but may have eternal life." In the Old Testament, God gave Abraham a similar test to see if he was willing to sacrifice his only son.

As you read this story, pay attention to why God blesses Abraham after this event.

Abraham and his wife Sarah had waited many years to have their son Isaac. They were very grateful to God for the gift of their son.

Then one day, God called Abraham. "Here I am," Abraham replied.

"Take your son, your only son Isaac, whom you love, and offer him as a sacrifice on a mountain," God told him.

Abraham woke up early in the morning and gathered wood to make a burnt offering. He took his son, and they traveled to the mountain where God had told him to go.

"Father!" Isaac said.

"Here I am, my son," Abraham replied.

"The fire and the wood are here, but where is the lamb for the sacrifice?" he asked.

"God himself will provide the lamb for the sacrifice, my son," Abraham replied.

When they arrived at the spot for the sacrifice, Abraham built an altar and laid the wood for the sacrifice. He tied up his son and laid him on the altar for the sacrifice.

Then the Lord sent an angel to stop him.

"Abraham, Abraham," the Lord called from heaven.

"Here I am," he said.

"Do not lay your hand on the boy or do anything to him; for now I know that you fear God, since you have not withheld your only son from me," God said.

Abraham looked up and saw a ram whose horns were caught in a bush. Abraham took the ram and sacrificed it as a burnt offering instead of his son. Abraham called the place "the Lord will provide."

God spoke to Abraham again, saying, "Because you have done this and have not withheld your only son, I will indeed bless you. I will make your children and descendants as numerous as the stars in heaven and as the sand that is on the seashore."

REFLECTION QUESTIONS

Why did God bless Abraham?

God did not withhold his only Son Jesus, whom he loved, as a sacrifice for us. Why should we give thanks to him when we offer the bread and wine as a sacrifice at Mass?

What things (not people) do we own that we can give up or sacrifice to show God how much we love and trust him?

THE PASSOVER FEAST

Exodus 11–13

The Jewish Passover feast celebrates God freeing the people of Israel from slavery in Egypt. This is the feast that Jesus commemorated with his disciples at the Last Supper when he instituted the Eucharist.

As you read this story, pay attention to the way God tells the Israelites to prepare the bread.

Moses had tried to convince Pharaoh, the king of Egypt, to free the Israelites without success. So God sent many plagues against Egypt to convince Pharaoh to free them. The plagues caused people to get sick or lose their crops and livestock. Each time, Moses tried to warn Pharaoh that there would be more plagues, but he did not listen.

Finally, God said to Moses, "I will send one more plague, and afterward Pharaoh will finally let you go. Not only that, but he will force you to leave."

Moses tried to warn Pharaoh one last time, saying, "Every firstborn in the land of Egypt will die, including your son who sits on the throne, if you do not let us go." The king would not listen.

The Lord gave Moses instructions to share with the people: "Each family must sacrifice a lamb and eat of it. The lamb must be a year-old male without any blemishes. Then they shall take the blood and spread it across the doorways to their homes. The blood shall be a sign, and I will pass over your homes when I see it. No plague shall destroy you. Cook the lamb, and eat all of it that night or burn what is left."

God also told Moses how they were to celebrate to remember this night in the years ahead. He told him they would eat unleavened bread for seven days. Unleavened bread is like a flat cracker. Normally, bread takes time to rise before it is cooked, because of the leaven, which is also called yeast.

The unleavened bread served to remind the people of what happened during the Passover. The firstborn in Egypt were killed, but the Israelites were spared. Pharaoh woke up in the middle of the night and cried out in fear and sorrow. He immediately summoned Moses and his brother Aaron. "Go away, both you and the Israelites! Go worship your God! Be gone and bring a blessing on me, too!"

Then the Egyptians urged the Israelites to leave immediately. This is why the Lord commanded them to celebrate with unleavened bread. They left so quickly that they could not even give their bread enough time to rise before packing it for their trip. With that, the Israelites went in haste out of the land of Egypt.

REFLECTION QUESTIONS

What did the Israelites eat to commemorate the Passover feast, and why?

In what ways is our paschal feast during Mass similar to the Passover feast commanded by God in the Old Testament?

THE MANNA IN THE DESERT

Exodus 16:1–21; Numbers 11:4–9

After the Israelites were freed from Egypt, they wandered in the wilderness. God provided for them a bread from heaven called manna when they were hungry.

As you read this story, pay attention to the instructions that God gives to the people about gathering the manna each day.

The Israelites were glad to be freed from slavery in Egypt, but as they wandered the wilderness, they started to realize how much they missed the comforts they had left behind. They were hungry. They started to grumble.

"Remember the fish we used to eat in Egypt? Remember the cucumbers, melons, onions, and tasty garlic we had? If only we had meat to eat!" they said.

So the people went to Moses and Aaron to voice their complaints. "Did you bring us out of Egypt into this wilderness to die of hunger?" they asked.

Then God spoke to Moses, saying, "I am going to rain down bread from heaven for my people. Each morning, they must go out and gather enough to last only for one day and no more."

So Moses and Aaron went to the Israelites and said, "In the morning, you will see the glory of the Lord, because he heard your complaints. Your complaining is not against us but against the Lord."

The next morning, when the wet dew on the grass lifted, the Israelites saw a flaky substance that looked like frost.

"What is it?" the people asked Moses.

"It is the manna. This is the bread that the Lord has given you to eat," Moses replied. "The Lord commands you to go out each morning and gather only what you need for the day and no more."

Some of the Israelites didn't listen. They worried that the manna would not be there the next day. They did not have faith in the Lord. When they took more than they needed, God punished the people for their lack of faith, and the leftover manna went bad.

As they continued to wander through the wilderness, the Israelites survived on the bread sent from heaven.

REFLECTION QUESTIONS

Why did the Israelites complain in the wilderness?

Why did some of the Israelites take more manna than they needed each day?

When do you worry that there will not be enough food, toys, time, money, or other things for yourself? How can you have faith that God will help you?

THE TESTIMONY OF JOHN THE BAPTIST

John 1:19–37

John the Baptist was one of the most well-known preachers in Judea. He had many followers. In this gospel story, the first followers of Jesus leave John the Baptist to follow Jesus instead.

As you read this story, pay attention to the way John the Baptist identifies Jesus to his disciples.

The Pharisees in Jerusalem sent people out to find John the Baptist to ask him questions.

"Who are you?" they asked.

"I am not the Messiah," John told them.

"What, then? Are you Elijah? Are you a prophet?" they asked.

"I am the voice of one crying out in the wilderness, 'Make straight the way of the Lord,'" he replied, referring to a prophecy in the book of Isaiah.

"I baptize with water, but among you stands the one who is coming after me. I am not worthy to untie his sandals," he said to them.

The next day, John the Baptist saw Jesus coming toward him.

"Here is the Lamb of God, who takes away the sin of the world!" he exclaimed. "This is he of whom I said, 'After me comes a man who ranks ahead of me, because he was before me.'"

Then John testified, "God sent me to baptize with water and said to me, 'He on whom you see the Spirit descend and remain is the one who baptizes with the Holy Spirit.' And I myself have seen and testified that this is the Son of God."

Then the next day, John was standing with two of his disciples, and he saw Jesus walk by again. "Look, here is the Lamb of God!" he exclaimed.

The two disciples heard him say this, and they left John to follow Jesus.

REFLECTION QUESTIONS

How did John the Baptist describe Jesus to the Pharisees and to his disciples?

What are some sins that the Lamb of God will take away through the Eucharist for kids your age?

If someone were to ask you about Jesus, what testimony would you give to explain who he is?

THE WEDDING FEAST AT CANA

John 2:1–12

Jesus performed his first miracle at a wedding feast before he became well-known throughout Judea. He was hesitant at first but then took the opportunity to show the glory of God.

As you read this story, pay attention to the miracle Jesus performs and what happens afterward.

There was a wedding in the town of Cana in Galilee. Jesus and his disciples were invited, and so was Jesus's mother.

During the wedding celebration, they ran out of wine. Mary went up to Jesus to tell him about it.

"They have no wine," she said to him.

"Woman, what concern is that to you and to me? My hour has not yet come," he said.

Mary ignored him. She went to the servants at the wedding and said, "Do whatever he tells you."

Jesus, being a good son, listened to his mother. He told the servants, "Fill six stone jars with water."

Each jar could hold twenty or thirty gallons of water. The servants filled them to the brim as Jesus had told them to do.

"Now draw some out, and take it to the chief steward," he told them.

The servants did as Jesus asked. The steward took a taste, but the water had become wine. He didn't know where the wine had come from, so he went to the groom of the wedding and said, "Everyone serves the good wine first and the wine that doesn't taste as good at the end of the party. Why have you saved the good wine until now?"

Jesus had turned the water into wine. It was the first miracle he performed to reveal his glory. After seeing this, the disciples believed in him.

REFLECTION QUESTIONS

What sign did Jesus perform to make his disciples believe in him?

What miracle does Jesus perform during Mass with the wine on the altar?

How can we do a better job listening to our mothers (and fathers) like Jesus did in this story?

What signs help you believe in Jesus?

THE DINNER WITH SINNERS

Matthew 9:9–13; Luke 5:27–32; Mark 2:13–17

Jesus Christ was the holy Son of God, yet he spent much of his time with sinful and unclean people. He touched and healed the sick and outcasts of the community and went into the homes of sinful people like tax collectors.

As you read this story, pay attention to the response Jesus gives to the people who criticize him for having dinner with tax collectors.

The people in Judea hated tax collectors. They hated them because they were thieves. They collected more money than they needed to pay to the Roman emperor and would keep the rest for themselves.

Jesus was walking one day, when he saw a man named Matthew (who was also called Levi) sitting at the tax booth where he worked.

Jesus looked to him and said, "Follow me."

Matthew got up and left his booth and followed Jesus without any hesitation. Matthew invited Jesus and his disciples to dinner in his home. He also invited his other tax collector friends to join them for dinner.

The people who saw Jesus enter into Matthew's home with these sinful tax collectors were shocked. The Pharisees, who were experts in the law and were respected men in the community, pulled some of the disciples aside to talk to them.

"Why does your teacher eat with tax collectors and sinners?" they asked.

Jesus heard them and got up from the dinner to speak with the Pharisees. "Those who are well do not need a doctor, but the sick do," he said. "I have not come to call the righteous, for they are already healthy. I come to call the sinners to change their lives, for they are like the sick, who need a doctor to heal them."

REFLECTION QUESTIONS

Why did Jesus eat dinner with Matthew and the sinful tax collectors?

Who are the kinds of people that Jesus would dine with today? Which table would he sit at in your school lunchroom?

How can you be more welcoming to people who come to share in the Eucharistic meal on Sundays?

THE PARABLE OF THE GREAT FEAST

Luke 14:15–24

Jesus told many parables about the kingdom of God and the people who would join him in his kingdom. Many people who heard these parables were surprised by what they heard.

As you read this story, pay attention to the people who accept the invitation to the great feast.

Jesus dined at the house of one of the leaders of the Pharisees. Many other people came to join them for the feast. One of the guests announced, "Blessed is anyone who will eat bread in the kingdom of God!"

Then Jesus told them a parable:

An important man gave a great dinner and invited many people. He sent out a servant to personally invite these people to the feast.

"Come, join us. The feast is ready now," the servant said to them.

But each one came up with a different excuse for not attending the dinner.

The first one said, "I have bought a piece of land, and I must go out and see it. Please accept my regrets."

Another invited guest said, "I have just bought oxen for my farm, and I am going to go try them out. Please accept my regrets."

A third person said, "I have just been married, and therefore I cannot come."

The servant returned and reported these excuses to his master, who became very angry.

"Go out at once into the streets and bring in the poor, the crippled, the blind, and the lame," he said to his servant.

He did what his master told him and returned to say, "Sir, I have brought in the people that you asked, but there is still room for more."

"Go out into the roads outside the town and convince the outcasts to come in so that my house may be filled. For I tell you, none of those who were invited will taste my dinner."

REFLECTION QUESTIONS

Who accepted the invitation to the great dinner?

What are some common reasons people want to skip Mass?

Who do you think are the kinds of people Jesus would want you to invite to join in the feast of the kingdom of God today?

THE FEEDING OF THE FIVE THOUSAND

Matthew 14:13–21; Mark 6:30–44; Luke 9:10–17; John 6:1–15

The news of Jesus's miracles and teachings spread quickly throughout Judea. Large crowds began to follow him to hear what he had to say and see what he would do.

As you read this story, pay attention to what the disciples say and do before Jesus performs the miracle of multiplying the bread.

Jesus invited his apostles to spend some quiet time alone with him. "Come away to a deserted place all by yourselves and rest with me for a while," he said.

So Jesus and his apostles went off to find a place for them to be alone. But a large crowd of people saw them leaving. They followed Jesus and his apostles.

When Jesus saw the many people following him, he felt compassion in his heart. "They are like sheep without a shepherd," he said. He welcomed them and began to teach them and heal those that were sick.

The apostles, however, were still tired and hoping for that quiet time alone with Jesus. As the day grew late, they came to Jesus and said, "Send the people away so they can go to the surrounding villages and country-side to buy something for themselves to eat."

Jesus smiled and said to his apostles, "You give them something to eat."

The apostles looked upon the large crowd of people, numbering at least five thousand men and their fami-lies. "We do not have enough money to buy that much bread for them," they said to Jesus.

"How many loaves do you have?" Jesus asked. "Go and see."

The apostles went and found a young boy there who had food with him. They returned to Jesus and said, "There is a boy here who has five loaves of bread and two fish. But what are they among so many?"

"Have everyone sit down in groups of about fifty people," Jesus instructed his apostles. They did so and returned to him.

Jesus took the five loaves and two fish and looked up to heaven. He blessed the bread and broke up the loaves and gave them to his disciples to distribute to the crowd.

The apostles traveled among the crowds of people, distributing the broken pieces of bread to the thou-sands of people there.

When they had finished, they gathered up what was left into twelve baskets of broken pieces of bread.

It was a miracle. With only five loaves of bread and two fish, Jesus and the apostles fed thousands and thousands of people.

REFLECTION QUESTIONS

What were the apostles worried about?

What about this story reminds you of the way we celebrate the Eucharist at Mass?

Jesus invited the apostles to go with him to find a deserted place to rest. When and where can you spend time with Jesus during your day?

THE BREAD OF LIFE

John 6:22-68

After the miraculous feeding of more than five thousand people, the crowds came in search of Jesus to learn more from him. When they found him, they had a lot of questions for him.

As you read this story, pay attention to the words that turn so many people away from Jesus.

It took the crowd of people some time before they could find Jesus after he miraculously fed the five thousand people. They had heard of his many other miracles, too, and went to follow him. When they finally found him, they asked, "Rabbi, when did you come here?"

Jesus replied, "Very truly, I tell you, you are looking for me because you ate your fill of the bread. Do not work for the food of this world, but for the food that endures for eternal life. The Son of Man will give this to you."

"What sign are you going to give us, so that we may see it and believe you?" they asked him. "Our ancestors ate manna in the wilderness. God gave them bread to eat."

Jesus replied, "It is my Father who gives you true bread from heaven. The bread of God that comes down from heaven gives life to the world."

"Sir, give us this bread always," they shouted.

"I am the bread of life. Whoever comes to me will never be hungry, and whoever believes in me will never be thirsty," Jesus said.

The Jews among the crowd began to complain. "Is not this Jesus, the son of Joseph, whose father and mother we know? How can he say he has come down from heaven?"

Jesus heard this and answered them, "Do not complain among yourselves. No one can come to me unless the Father wills it, and I will raise that person on the last day."

Jesus repeated again, "I am the bread of life. Your ancestors ate manna in the wilderness, but they died. This is the bread that comes down from heaven. If you eat of it, you will not die. The bread that I will give for the life of the world is my flesh."

The Jews argued among themselves, saying, "How can this man give us his flesh to eat?"

Jesus said to them, "Unless you eat the flesh of the Son of Man and drink his blood, you have no life within you. Those who eat my flesh and drink my blood have eternal life, and I will raise them up on the last day."

His disciples heard this and said, "This teaching is difficult; who can accept it?"

"Does this offend you?" Jesus asked them. "The words that I have spoken to you are spiritual but true. They will give you life. But among you there are some who do not believe."

When his disciples heard this, many of them turned back home. They no longer wanted to follow Jesus.

"Do you also wish to go away?" Jesus asked his twelve apostles.

"Lord, to whom can we go? You have the words of eternal life," the apostle Peter replied.

REFLECTION QUESTIONS

What did Jesus say that led some of the crowd and even his disciples to turn away and leave him?

Based on these teachings, why should you eat the bread of life and drink Jesus's blood?

When you are unsure of the teachings of Jesus or the Church, who do you go to for help with understanding?

THE HEALING OF THE CENTURION'S SERVANT

Matthew 8:5–13

Right before we receive communion at Mass, we pray, "Lord, I am not worthy that you should enter under my roof, but only say the word and my soul shall be healed." This prayer comes from the story of the Roman centurion asking Jesus to heal his servant.

As you read this story, pay attention to the respect that the centurion shows Jesus, even though he is not Jewish or one of Jesus's followers.

The Romans ruled over Israel. The Roman emperor sent soldiers to watch over the people and make sure they would obey him. A centurion was a commander of one hundred soldiers in the Roman army. As Jesus entered Capernaum, a Roman centurion approached him, pleading for help.

"Lord, my servant is lying at home, paralyzed and in terrible distress," he said.

Jesus replied, "I will come and cure him."

The centurion was surprised by the response. "Lord, I am not worthy to have you come under my roof, but only speak the word and my servant will be healed." The centurion straightened his uniform and stood a little bit taller and said, "I am also a man with authority, with many soldiers under me. I say to one, 'Go,' and he goes, and to another, 'Come,' and he comes."

Jesus was amazed by the centurion's words. "Truly, I tell you, in no one in Israel have I found such faith. Many will come from outside of Israel to eat with Abraham and Isaac and Jacob in the kingdom of heaven, while those who reject me will be thrown into darkness."

Jesus turned to the centurion and said, "Go; let it be done for you according to your faith."

The centurion's servant was healed in that hour.

REFLECTION QUESTIONS

How did the Roman centurion show respect for Jesus?

How can we strengthen our faith and better prepare to receive Jesus into our bodies at Mass?

In what ways do you or people you know need the healing power of Jesus?

THE LAST SUPPER

Matthew 26:26–30; Mark 14:22–26; Luke 22:14–20

On the night before he died, Jesus celebrated the Passover feast with his disciples. There, he instituted a new kind of feast for them to celebrate to remember him and what he did for them. This story tells the origin of the Eucharist and the celebration of communion we share at church.

As you read the story, pay attention to the way he describes his Body (the bread) and his Blood (the wine).

While they were eating the Passover feast, Jesus picked up a piece of bread, gave thanks, and said a blessing. He broke it and gave it to his disciples, saying, "Take this and eat, for this is my body, which will be given up for you. Do this in remembrance of me."

Then he took the cup and gave thanks. He gave the cup to them to share and said, "Drink this, all of you, for this is my blood, the blood of the new covenant, which is poured out for many for the forgiveness of sins."

Then they all gathered together to sing a hymn and went out to a mountain to pray.

REFLECTION QUESTIONS

What would happen to Jesus's Body and Blood after the Last Supper?

How do you remember this meal at your church?

How can we make a gift of our lives to others like Jesus did?

THE WASHING OF THE DISCIPLES' FEET

John 13:1–20

During the Last Supper, Jesus wanted to give his disciples one last gift before he died, so he washed their feet.

As you read this story, pay attention to the way the disciples react to Jesus washing their feet.

After celebrating the Passover feast with his disciples, Jesus got up and took off his outer robe. He took a towel and wrapped it around his waist. He found a bowl and poured water into it.

Then he did something shocking. He went from disciple to disciple, kneeling down and washing each of their feet. He scrubbed their feet clean and dried them with his towel.

He came to Peter, who said, "Lord, are you really going to wash my feet?"

"Later you will understand," Jesus replied.

"You will never wash my feet," Peter said.

"Unless I wash your feet, you will have no share with me," Jesus said.

He finished washing their feet and put on his robe again. He returned to the table and said to them, "Do you know what I have done for you? You call me 'Teacher' and 'Lord,' and rightly so, for I am indeed. So if I, your Teacher and Lord, washed your feet, you must also wash one another's feet. I am setting an example for you to follow. As I have done, so you should also do."

REFLECTION QUESTIONS

How would you feel if you were one of the disciples and Jesus washed your feet?

In what ways do priests and other ministers humbly serve the people of God?

While you may not wash other people's feet, how can you humbly serve your friends, family, and other people you know?

THE PIERCING OF JESUS'S SIDE

John 19:31–37

Art and sculptures of Jesus's body on the cross show the wounds on his hands, feet, and side. This is the story of why Jesus's side was cut during his crucifixion.

As you read this story, pay attention to what comes out of Jesus's side after it is pierced.

After a great amount of suffering, Jesus died on the cross. The holy Sabbath day was approaching, and this was the day of the week when the Jews rested. So the Jews asked the Roman governor, Pilate, to remove the bodies from the crosses before the Sabbath.

He ordered the soldiers to break the legs of the men being crucified to make sure they would all be dead by sundown. So the soldiers went down the line of crosses, breaking the legs of the men hanging on each one.

But when they came to Jesus, the soldiers could see he was already dead. So one of them took a spear and cut Jesus on his side to be sure. Blood and water came out.

There was a Christian there to witness these events. He was amazed because he knew the scripture passages that said, "none of his bones would be broken" and "they will look on the one whom they have pierced." He told many people about this event, including Saint John, who recorded the events in his Gospel.

REFLECTION QUESTIONS

What came out of Jesus's side after it was pierced on the cross?

Why do you think Christians connect this event to the sacraments of Baptism and the Eucharist?

What have you seen as an eyewitness during Mass that you can tell others about during the week?

THE ROAD TO EMMAUS

Luke 24:13–35

After Jesus rose from the dead, he appeared to many of his disciples. He encountered two of these disciples shortly after his death and resurrection just outside of Jerusalem. They were traveling on the road to a village called Emmaus.

As you read this story, pay attention to the way the disciples finally realize that it was Jesus who was with them.

It was a difficult few days for the disciples of Jesus. They had seen and heard about the death of their Lord. Two of these disciples left the city of Jerusalem, where Jesus was crucified, and began to walk the seven miles to a village called Emmaus.

They were walking along the road, talking about all that had happened, when Jesus came near and began to walk with them.

"What are you talking about while you walk along the road?" Jesus asked.

They stopped and looked at one another in sadness, asking, "Are you the only one in Jerusalem who does not know the things that have taken place these last few days?"

"What things?" Jesus asked.

"The things about Jesus of Nazareth and how our chief priests and leaders handed him over to be crucified," said one of the disciples.

"We had hoped that he would be the one to redeem Israel. Today is the third day since he died," said the other disciple.

The first disciple jumped in and said, "Moreover, some women of our group have astounded us. They were at his tomb this morning, and they did not find his body there. They told us they had a vision of angels who said he was alive!"

"Others went to the tomb and found it just as the women had said, but they did not see him," said the other disciple.

"Oh, how foolish you are, and slow of heart to believe all that the prophets declared!" Jesus said. "It was necessary that the Messiah should suffer these things and enter into his glory."

Then as they continued to walk, Jesus interpreted many things that the prophets, beginning with Moses, had said about him in the scriptures.

Finally, they arrived in the village of Emmaus, and Jesus walked ahead of them.

"Stay with us! It is almost evening, and the day is now nearly over," the disciples shouted.

So Jesus came back to stay with them. They sat down for a meal, and Jesus took bread, blessed and broke it, and gave it to the disciples.

At that moment, their eyes were opened, and they recognized Jesus for the first time. Then he vanished from their sight.

They turned to each other. "Were not our hearts burning within us while he was explaining the scriptures to us?"

They got up immediately and returned to Jerusalem to tell the apostles about their encounter with Christ.

REFLECTION QUESTIONS

When did the disciples finally recognize Jesus?

Who helps you understand the scriptures?

How can you show more reverence (holy respect) when in the presence of Jesus Christ in the Eucharist?

THE FEEDING OF THE SHEEP

John 21:15–19

After he rose from the dead, Jesus appeared to his apostles. During one of these appearances, he spoke with Peter, the leader of the apostles.

As you read this story, pay attention to what Jesus asks Peter to do to show his love for him.

Jesus appeared to his disciples while they were fishing on the Sea of Galilee. He invited them to share a meal with him. After the meal, Jesus spoke with Simon Peter.

"Peter, do you love me more than my other disciples?" Jesus asked.

"Yes, Lord; you know that I love you," Peter replied.

"Feed my lambs," Jesus said.

Then a second time, Jesus asked him, "Peter, do you love me?"

"Yes, Lord; you know that I love you," he replied again.

"Tend my sheep," Jesus said to him.

Jesus said to him a third time, "Do you love me?"

Peter was hurt that Jesus had asked this so many times. "Lord, you know everything. You know that I love you," he said

Jesus said to him, "Feed my sheep. Very truly, I tell you, when you were younger, you used to get dressed yourself and go wherever you wished. But when you grow old, you will rely on others to help you get dressed, and they will take you where you do not wish to go."

Jesus said this to warn Peter about his death one day. Peter would be crucified and killed many years later.

After this, Jesus said, "Follow me."

REFLECTION QUESTIONS

What did Jesus ask Peter to do? Who are the lambs and sheep that Peter fed after Jesus ascended to heaven?

How do priests show Jesus they love him by feeding the flocks of sheep in their churches?

How can we show Jesus we love him in our daily lives?

THE FIRST CONVERTS

Acts 2

After Jesus rose from the dead and ascended into heaven, the apostles carried on his mission with the help of the Holy Spirit. Peter was the first apostle to address the crowds of people after the coming of the Spirit.

As you read this story, pay attention to what the first converts did after their baptisms.

The apostles gathered together in a house in Jerusalem after Jesus had ascended into heaven. A strong wind blew through the house, and tongues of fire appeared among them. They began to speak in many other languages.

Many devout Jews from all over the world lived in Jerusalem. They heard the sound of the violent wind and came to investigate. They found the apostles filled with the Holy Spirit and speaking in the languages that they could each understand. Then Peter addressed the crowds and told them about the life, death, and resurrection of Jesus Christ.

Peter's words touched the hearts of the people. "Brothers, what should we do?" they said to him and the other apostles.

"Repent and be baptized in the name of Jesus Christ so that your sins may be forgiven, and you will receive the gift of the Holy Spirit," Peter said in reply.

Three thousand people were baptized that day and joined the new Christian community. They devoted themselves to the teachings of the apostles. They gathered together to pray and for a celebration of the Eucharist by the breaking of bread.

These new converts also supported each other financially. They shared their possessions and gave money to anyone in their community who had need of it.

Day by day, the Lord added new members to this community of people who were being saved.

REFLECTION QUESTIONS

After they converted to Christianity, what did the people do together to worship God?

The early Christians shared their possessions with those who needed them the most. What things do you share most often with others at home or at school?

How can you support the other members of your Christian community with time, possessions, or money?

THE BREAKING OF THE BREAD

1 Corinthians 11:17–34

Saint Paul wrote letters to many churches that he had founded. He often wrote with instructions for how to live within Christian communities.

As you read this story, pay attention to the instructions Paul gives to the Corinthians about how to prepare to receive the Body and Blood of Christ.

The Corinthians were a new community of Christians and still learning the best way to support one another and worship God. Paul was one of their leaders, and he wrote a letter to help them become better Christians while he traveled.

In this letter, he reminded them of what they celebrate when they come together to break the bread. He told them the story of the Last Supper and how Jesus said, "Do this in memory of me."

Some of the Corinthians were eating more than their fair share of the bread. Some of them were drinking so much of the wine that they became drunk. Paul was not happy about this.

"Don't you have homes to eat and drink in?" he wrote to them. "If you are hungry, eat at home. Whoever eats the bread or drinks the cup of the Lord in an unworthy manner will be answerable for the body and blood of the Lord."

He gave them a challenge, writing, "Examine yourselves, and only then eat of the bread and drink of the cup."

He had many other things to say to them about this, but he wrote that he would instruct them more when he returned to visit their church.

REFLECTION QUESTIONS

What advice did Paul give to the Corinthians about receiving the body and blood of Christ?

How can you prepare yourself to eat the bread and drink the cup of the Lord in a worthy manner?

THE LAMB OF GOD

God gave John a vision of the heavens that he recorded in the book of Revelation. In this vision, he saw Jesus in the form of a lamb. Lambs were sacrificed by God's people in the Old Testament for forgiveness of sins. The blood of a lamb was also used during the Passover.

As you read this story, pay attention to the words of the song that the angels and saints sing to the Lamb of God.

John saw the Lord sitting on a throne holding a scroll with seven seals and an angel proclaiming in a loud voice, "Who is worthy to open the scroll and break its seals?"

John looked around. There was no one there in heaven or on earth that was worthy to open the scroll or look into it. This made John weep.

Then he saw a lamb standing before the scroll. The lamb went and took the scroll from the right hand of the one on the throne.

All the creatures and elders in heaven bowed down before the lamb. They held harps and bowls full of incense to offer their prayers to God.

They sang a new song, which began, "You are worthy to take the scroll and to open its seals."

Then John heard the voices of the thousands of angels surrounding the throne joining in a song:

"Worthy is the Lamb that was slain to receive power and wealth and wisdom and might and honor and glory and blessing!"

Then the song continued, and every creature in heaven and earth joined in singing:

"To the one seated on the throne of the Lamb be blessing and honor and glory and might for ever and ever!"

Then they ended their song and said, "Amen!"

REFLECTION QUESTIONS

What did the angels and saints sing about the Lamb of God?

How can we give Jesus (the Lamb of God) honor and glory in our lives?

ABOUT BIBLE BREAKS

The Bible Breaks stories for kids help families and faith formation groups set aside a few minutes during the day to read and reflect on the Word of God. Each short and simple story is written to help teach children the most important lessons of the Christian life from sacred Scripture.

To learn more and see the other Bible story collections in the series, visit:

jareddees.com/biblebreaks

You can also sign up for a weekly email newsletter featuring a new Bible story for kids every week.

ALSO BY JARED DEES

Jared Dees is the author of numerous books, including a short story collection titled *Beatitales: 80 Fables about the Beatitudes for Children*.

Download a collection of these stories at jareddees.com/beatitales.

MORE BOOKS BY JARED DEES

31 Days to Becoming a Better Religious Educator

To Heal, Proclaim, and Teach

Praying the Angelus

Christ in the Classroom

Beatitales

Tales of the Ten Commandments

Do Not Be Afraid

ABOUT THE AUTHOR

Jared Dees is the creator of *TheReligionTeacher.com*, a popular website that provides practical resources and teaching strategies to religious educators. A respected graduate of the Alliance for Catholic Education (ACE) program at the University of Notre Dame, Dees holds master's degrees in education and theology, both from Notre Dame. He frequently gives keynotes and leads workshops at conferences, church events, and school in-services throughout the year on a variety of topics. He lives near South Bend, Indiana, with his wife and children.

Learn more about Jared's books, speaking events, and other projects at jareddees.com.